I0158901

He Didn't Throw the Clay Away

Nate Fortner

Whosoever Press

He Didn't Throw the Clay Away

Whosoever
Press

Whosoever Press books may be ordered through booksellers or by contacting:

Whosoever Press
P.O. Box 1513
Boaz, Alabama 35957
www.WhosoeverPress.com

www.NateFortnerMinistries.webs.com
256-706-3315

All scripture quatations are from the NKJV.

ISBN-13: 978-0615857411 (sc)

Printed in the United States of America

Whosoever Press rev. date: 07/27/2013

He's the Potter
and We're the Clay

Jeremiah 18:1-6 says the word which came to Jeremiah from the LORD, saying: "Arise and go down to the potter's house, and there I will cause you to hear My words." Then I went down to the potter's house, and there he was, making something at the wheel. And the vessel that he made of clay was marred in the hand of the potter; so he made it again into another vessel, as it seemed good to the potter to make. Then the word of the LORD came to me, saying: "O house of Israel, can I not do with you as this potter?" says the LORD. "Look, as the clay *is* in the potter's hand, so *are* you in My hand, O house of Israel! Isaiah 64:8 says But now, O LORD, You *are* our Father; we *are* the clay, and You our potter; and all we *are* the work of Your hand.

The Bible is clear in these verses that we are the workmanship of the very hands of God Himself. He is referred to as a Potter sitting at a wheel spinning the clay and forming it into a beautiful piece of art. That clay is us as humans.

Genesis 1:26-28 says Then God said, "Let us make man in Our image, according to Our likeness; let them have dominion over the fish of the sea, over the birds of the air, and over the cattle, over all the earth and over every creeping thing that creeps on the earth." So God created man in His *own* image; in the image of God He created him; male and female He created them. Then God blessed them, and God said to them, "Be fruitful and multiply; fill the earth and subdue it; have dominion over the fish of the sea, over the birds of the air, and over every living thing that moves on the earth." Genesis 2:7 says "And the LORD God formed man *of* the dust of the ground, and breathed into his nostrils the breath of life; and man became a living being."

We've all heard the Genesis account of Creation at some point in our lives. We know that God said, "Let's make man in our image." Who was He speaking about? In Our image? Himself, Jesus, and the Holy Spirit. So we know by this that even though God is a Spirit, He has hands, feet, eyes, a nose, and every part that we as humans have. It was His desire for us to be created in His image! Not even the angels have that testimony. God wanted us to be uniquely different than any other creature that He had created. On the first six days of Creation, He created everything; the earth, planets, stars moons, plants, and even the animals. On the sixth day, God created man; male and female.

Pottery and Terms to Know

Before a masterpiece can be created, it takes some time for preparation. Whether you're an artist, musician, or even a sports player, it takes practice to be great. It's possible that the artist could paint hundreds of landscapes before they get that one that just takes the world by surprise. It's truly amazing when we hear a new song on the radio that completely drenches our spirit. Then, when we see a TV interview with the song's writer, we get to hear the testimony of how God gave them that breathtaking song. Growing up in Huntington, West Virginia, I saw the Marshall University Football team practice every weekend. Football players such as Chad Pennington and Byron Leftwich had to put in many years of practice to perfect their game. It the same manner, whatever you decide to do with your life, it most likely won't happen without many weeks, months, or even years of study and practice.

When it comes to pottery, you have to know how to mold and shape the clay to make it hold its shape. Whether you work on a spinning wheel or simply mold the clay in your hand, it takes some preparation time to get the clay ready. You can either purchase the clay premade, in powder form, or dig it up in your back yard. However you decide is up to you.

Once you get your clay formed, you have to wedge the clay. This is where you throw it down on a surface such as a canvas for painting. The canvas will make it easier to peel off. The length of time you spend wedging your clay is up to you. The clay needs to be flexible and easy to mold. The purpose of wedging the clay is to get the bubbles out of the clay. To see the bubbles in the clay, mold a ball of clay and cut it in half with a piece of fishing line. Bubbles in your clay could cause the finished art to explode in the kiln while it is being fired.

Scoring your clay is another important process if you plan on connecting two separate pieces of clay together to make one piece. Scoring is as simple as taking the prongs of a table fork and scratching up the particular area where you plan to join the two pieces of clay. You will need to score both pieces of clay to make the connection a success.

Only when you have done all the preparation work and have sat down at the

Potter's Wheel, are you are ready to create your masterpiece. Now you've placed your clay on the wheel and you've started spinning the wheel. You need to add a little water to the clay periodically to keep it wet and moist. Keeping the clay wet and moist will help you to mold and shape your art easier. However, if you every let the clay get too dry or off center, then the clay can get marred up! When the clay gets marred up, that means it has fallen apart and flew off the spinning wheel. Sometimes the clay lands on the floor after it gets marred up and then the clay isn't good for anything. What happens now? You have two choices: Either throw the clay away or clean any dirt off and start the whole preparation process over again.

Jesus Likes Playing in the Dirt

Jeremiah 29:11 tells us that God has plans for us! Plans to prosper us, to give us hope, and a future! 1 Corinthians 2:9 tells us that "Eye has not seen, nor ear heard, nor have entered into the heart of man the things which God has prepared for those who love Him." It's such a blessing to me to know that after all of my sin, Jesus still loves me! After all my faults and all my failures, Jesus still loves me! He is the Potter and we are the clay! I'm not perfect and I make mistakes, but it's like the song says, "Don't judge me yet, there's an unfinished part! He's still working on me!"

We read in Genesis 2:7 that God formed man out of the dust of the earth and then breathed into his nostrils the breath of life. Can you imagine in your mind, God molding and shaping the first man Adam out of the dust of the earth? This paints such a beautiful picture in my mind of how tender hearted our God truly is! On the first six days of Creation, God spoke everything into existence except one thing. Man! The Bible says God took the time mold and shape Adam out of the dust of the earth. He even had Jesus and the Holy Spirit there to help.

He said let *US* make man in *OUR* image! This proves that He wasn't alone! Can you imagine as the angels of heaven were all standing around watching to see what God was doing on the earth playing in the dirt? He didn't even take that much time creating them. They were spoken into existence as far as we know.

Matthew 19:14 says "But Jesus said, Suffer little children, and forbid them not, to come unto me: for of such is the kingdom of heaven." In other words, Jesus said let all the children come unto me! I love them! I know the very number of hairs they have upon their heads. I think of them so many times each day that it compares to the numbers of grains of sand on the sea shore. I can see Jesus in my mind now as He was speaking to the crowds when the children came unto Him. I know their hearts. My Kingdom is of such! No wonder Jesus said let the little children come unto Him! He knew their hearts better than anyone! I can see Him in my mind even now as He, the Father, and the Holy Spirit formed the first man Adam. I bet Jesus would get down on the ground with the kids and play in the dirt. If Jesus showed up to play with the kids now days, He'd be playing with Hot wheels and Matchbox cars making roads in the dirt. I guarantee you His mind would go back to Eden when He and the Father along with the Holy Spirit played in the dirt and formed man. God knows the hearts of our children better than anyone else!

Maybe you're Broken and Have Cracks, but Jesus Can Patch Them

The Bible says that He knew us in the womb. Before we were even born, He knew who we would be! The Holy Spirit then gave us our gifts, talents, and abilities that we would later be able to use to bring God glory! He molds each and every one of us into exactly who He would have us to be! That is, if we allow Him to! Sometimes we rebel and do things our own way. It's okay though because sometimes we as Christians mess up. Sometimes we say No to God and we choose our own paths. Sometimes we end up like that clay on the Potter's Wheel. We become dry and need a little bit of the moisture of the Holy Spirit! Sometimes we mess up and commit sins. We get marred up a little bit in the hands of Jesus. We get marred up because of our choices, but we're still in the Potter's hands! The most amazing thing is that He doesn't throw us away when we get marred up and dirty from the fall. He picks us up and begins to remold and reshape us again! He starts over! When you stumble and fall, Jesus picks up the pieces!

Just because you may have messed up in your past doesn't mean that it's over! I can see Jesus as He begins to wedge the clay again! He's making you a new creation! I'm so glad that Jesus doesn't determine my future based on the failures of my past! He said He would establish our end from the beginning! He's the Author and the Finisher of our faith! Jesus works out all the bubbles so we don't explode when we have to go through the fire! Jesus said, in this life you will face tribulations!

Sometimes in this life, we get hurt by those closest to us and this can cause cracks in our vessel. We are the vessel. We are the piece of art God is molding and shaping. When people try to hurt us or get us sidetracked, Jesus doesn't always keep us from going through that situation, but He promised He would be there to walk with us as we sail through the storms of life! Remember Jesus is the same yesterday, today and forever! That means He can still walk on the water even when the waves get high!

Dry and Burnt Out

When we get dry and burnt out, Jesus will add some water and smooth out the rough edges. We need the moisture of the Holy Spirit! When we face burn out, it's time for revival! We are the King's kids! We have royal blood flowing through our veins and one day we will reign and rule with Christ! When we face those dry spells in our lives, we have to remember who we are! We're not of this world! We're just Pilgrims passing through on our way to a better home!

We have to remember that He is the Great I AM! He's the Light of the World! He's the Door of the Sheep! He's the Good Shepherd! He is the Resurrection and the Life! He is the True Vine! He is the Way, the Truth and the Life! When you can't find your way, Jesus will be your Way! When you can find truth, Jesus will be your Truth! When you can't find out where you're going in this life, Jesus will be your life! He is the Author and the Finisher of our faith, and He's written the greatest book ever published! I've read it and we win!

In Luke 15:11-24, we read the story of the Prodigal Son. A father had two sons and the youngest came to him and said, "Father, give to me the portion of your house that will fall to me." I imagine the father was hurt. His vessel became cracked, but he divided his house unto both of his sons. Once the younger son was all packed he left home and the Bible says he travelled to a far off land and lived a life of riotous living. In other words, this teenage boy went wild and blew everything he had!

The Bible says the young boy began to be in want because he had run out of money. He was broke as a joke! A great famine had hit the land where he was living and so he had no choice but to become a hired worker and try to earn his meal each day. One day we read in the scripture that he finally came to his senses and went home to his father's house. What happened next is shoutin' material! He started walking home and while he was still a great way off the Bible says the father saw him and took off running to meet him! This is such a beautiful scene from a much larger picture! This is the one story in the Bible where we see God run! The father in this story represents God the Father, and He took off running down that long dusty road to meet his lost son. I believe many of us can relate to the story of the Prodigal Son because at one point in each of our lives, we were running from God. I believe it's this way every Sunday morning when a lost son repents and comes home. The Father in heaven comes running to welcome you back home!

We also read that when the father met the boy at the end of the road that he hugged him and kissed him. Then the father turned to those that were with him and said, "Put the best robe on him. Put a ring on his hand. Put sandals on his feet. Let's kill the fatted calf and celebrate! My son which was lost is now found!" When the father took off running to meet his son at the end of the road, the Bible says he turned to someone and spoke. Who was the father talking to? I'm guessing maybe some of the hired servants, since this story is symbolic to God the Father. That means, when a sinner repents, not only does God the Father run to meet them in the middle of their mess, but He turns and speaks to someone and says, "Go prepare to feast!" Who is God the Father speaking to? I believe it's the angels because in Luke 15:10 it says "Likewise, I say to you, there is joy in the presence of the angels of God over one sinner who repents." Have you ever thought about it though? We can sing the song of the redeemed! We are the redeemed, but the angels of God can't even sing the song that we get to sing!

If you read further into the story of the Prodigal Son, you will also read the account of the older son. He was in the field working when he overheard a loud noise that sounded like a celebration. When he called for one of the hired servants to tell him what it meant, the servant said "Your brother has come home and your father has killed the fatted calf to celebrate." Now the older son gets mad and goes to his father and says, "All these years I've served you, and you've never given me a calf to celebrate with my friends; but as soon as this rebellious wild child of your returns looking for a handout, you throw a party!"

I have to say, I can see the older brother's hurt. I can see where he's coming from. Even though the older son was home with his father, I believe he was stressed and depressed. He wanted to have fun, but felt like he had to work all the time. When he told his father he thought it was unfair, the father revealed a revelation that the oldest son had not seen! The father told him, "Everything I have is yours! You can have any calf you want! Have a feast with your friends anytime you please!" Even though in this story there are so many different emotions, I see salvation, family restoration, and a father's years of praying for that lost son to re-dedicate!

Even though this is a great story of redemption, this story goes even further. When the father said, "Let's celebrate," I believe this is also symbolic to the Marriage Supper of the Lamb. At the end of this age, we will either end up in heaven or hell. For all of us who enter heaven's gates we're going to feast! Celebration time in heaven! As the Father in the scripture gave gifts to his son who returned home and repented, the Bible says that when we get to heaven we will receive crowns with jewels.

All Men Fall, but the Great Ones Get Back Up

I'm reminded of another young man who left home at the age of twenty in the year 2005 and moved five hundred miles away! He gave away all his suits and ties and said he would no longer call himself a Christian! He still loved God and would always tell others about Jesus, but he wouldn't serve Him any longer. Many events led to him making that decision. I remember he left his family and life behind on Christmas Eve of 2005. He walked away and said he quit! This young man dried up and became a worthless piece of clay that was no good for anything, but Jesus saw a product name Nate Fortner worth paying a price for! The price was His own life on a cross, but Jesus said, "No, I won't let Nate's life end up like this!" Then Jesus started to wedge again! He started remolding and reshaping me again! I was dried up, marred up and ready to be tossed out, but JESUS in His mercy said No! He had a plan of redemption for Nate Fortner! I'm so thankful that He didn't throw this piece of clay away! He started over again!

I imagine seeing Jesus sitting playing in the dirt with His Father forming something beautiful in many people in America! I see revival coming! Joel 2:28 reminds me that God said in the last days He would pour out His Spirit upon all flesh!

Jesus knew we would mess up, but He said I'm going to make them new! No, they won't be perfect, but I AM! Yes, people are going to talk about you, I love you! You may have everybody in your phone book talking about you, but I'm declaring your name among the angels in heaven! You stand tall and proud of those cracks! You show off those battle scars because one day you'll trade them in for a crown of Victory! Don't be afraid to tell the world that you've been broken. You've fallen and you've messed up, but it's okay because all men fall! It's the great ones who get back up!

Just because you've messed up in the past doesn't mean that you can't come home to the Father! If God was through with you, He'd have thrown the clay away, but He said NO! I've got to keep this one here with me! There's still hope for you!

I figure that you or someone you may know has been going through the fire lately. Your clay may be marred up, but Jesus is in control! He didn't throw the clay away! He's waiting for you to make the move! Let Jesus shape you into a masterpiece! So many times we face the circumstances of life and when they don't go the way we plan, sometimes we take it out on God. You see there's one thing I've not told you yet about the Potter and the clay. Before the clay can become that beautiful piece of art work that God has determined for you to be, the clay must be put into the kiln. We must go through the fire sometimes, but remember that you're not alone! Shadrach, Meshach, and Abendego were thrown into the fiery furnace, Nebuccadnezar saw a fourth man walking in the midst of the fire who resembled the Son of God! Jesus will never fail us! He is continually forming and molding us into His likeness.

When we get saved, the Bible says we receive the Holy Spirit. Where two or more are gathered in Jesus name, He said He would be in the midst of them. We know that God the Father is Omnipresent! That means He's everywhere at once! The Bible also speaks of various types of angels. There are warring angels, Archangels, trumpet blowing angels, guardian angels, and more! There are angels that have been dispatched from heaven and assigned to you! No matter where you go or what you face, you've got a heavenly host backing you up everywhere you go! There's no way you can fail if you'll trust in Jesus!

Is Jesus the Lord of Your Life?

Have you ever accepted Jesus as your Lord and Savior? He loves you so much! If you're not a Christian and you would like to know Jesus in a more intimate way then simply pray and ask Him to forgive you of your sins. You must believe that Jesus lived, died on the cross and was raised from the grave on the third day! To pray to God, you simply talk to Him out loud and He will hear you even if you think He doesn't! He promised in the Bible that He would have His ears open and listening to you when you call on Him!

If you're still unsure how to pray and ask Jesus to save you and make you a Christian, then let me lead you in a prayer. If you will mean it in your heart and believe, you will be saved! Okay, repeat this prayer after me.

Dear Jesus,

Please forgive me of my sins. I know I've made mistakes and I must be born again. Jesus, I believe You died on the cross to carry my sins far away and that You rose again on the third day victorious over death, hell, and the grave! I will live for You the rest of my life, and by confessing my faith in You I am saved in Jesus name.

Amen.

If you just prayed this prayer, I would like to encourage you to get involved in a good Bible believing Church so you can learn more about Jesus. It will be good for you to fellowship with other Christians.

Please write to me and let me know about your Salvation today!

www.NateFortnerMinistries@yahoo.com

Or write to: Nate Fortner
P.O. Box 1513
Boaz, Alabama 35957

www.ingramcontent.com/pod-product-compliance
Lightning Source LLC
Chambersburg PA
CBHW060552030426
42337CB00019B/3522